Japan's Manufacturing Competitiveness Strategy: Challenges for Japan, Opportunities for the United States

by
Jane Corwin
and
Rebecca Puckett

INTERNATIONAL
T R A D E
ADMINISTRATION

Published April 2009 by the U.S. Department of Commerce, International Trade Administration.

The full text of this report is available on the International Trade Administration's Internet site at *www. trade.gov*. It is also available for purchase as a paper, microfiche, or electronic reprint from the National Technical Information Service, 5285 Port Royal Road, Springfield, VA 22161; *www.ntis.gov*.

Contents

Foreword

Because I was born in Japan to missionary parents and lived there until college, a goal of mine was to find a bridge between my past in Japan and my professional career at the U.S. Department of Commerce. I completed a temporary detail in the spring of 2007 to Japan that helped me to fulfill this goal. When I decided to do a detail to the U.S. Embassy in Japan, I explored possible areas of research in U.S.–Japan trade policy. After my consultations with ITA senior staff members, investigating Japan's manufacturing competitiveness strategy seemed like a needed project.

Because I had worked on the Department of Commerce's recent Manufacturing Strategy Initiative, I was keen to learn more about Japan's approach to competitiveness, especially in light of Japan's emergence from a period of lengthy economic stagnation.[1] How is Japan organizing itself to move to the next level of manufacturing technology and competitiveness to offset growth from China and the rest of Asia? Does the Japanese government have a roadmap for staying ahead of global competition? Does the private sector have a manufacturing strategy of its own?

Would I hear something different from successful U.S. companies in Japan? Was there a pattern to successful business models for foreign firms in the Japanese market?

If we ask those questions to a variety of industry and government insiders, a clearer picture of Japan's reformulated competitive strategy should emerge.

This project was not intended to be a thorough survey of Japanese industry or government agencies. Within a mere four weeks, just a snapshot—or glimpse—of what is happening in the manufacturing arena emerged. Drawing from close to 100 pages of my handwritten notes taken during interviews, I have presented only a sampling of case studies. What is summarized here is based, however, on what I heard and was redrafted from my extensive notes. The concepts are not mine, but they are conveyed through the interviews.

Jane Corwin
Director, Office of Trade Policy Analysis, Manufacturing and Services, International Trade Administration, U.S. Department of Commerce, Washington, D.C.

Executive Summary

After a 10-year period of economic stagnation, Japan is pursuing various tracks to promote the expansion of its economy and its manufacturing sector in particular. Japan is engaged in a cohesive "innovation program" at all levels: academia, government, and industry. There is a widespread belief in all sectors of Japan's economy that innovation will be the linchpin for improving productivity and for sustaining strong economic growth and global competitiveness. Innovation is viewed not only as technological invention, but also as a broad social transformation that enables ideas and discoveries with the creation of new social systems and values.

The Japanese government's science and technology (S&T) strategic roadmap and its manufacturing competitiveness strategy are inextricably linked, well coordinated and organized, consistent in focus and policy direction, and very well funded. The overall strategy according to those roadmaps includes a number of key components:

- Maintain various research funding levels according to the development stage of research and development (R&D).

- Build a sustainable and progressive industry–academia–government collaboration.

- Promote the use of new technologies in the public sector.

- Promote entrepreneurial activities and R&D ventures by private enterprises.

Japan's promotion of an active S&T strategy is designed to help jump-start innovation and to enable success in the manufacturing sector and the economy as a whole. In the minds of Japanese leaders, another key to Japan's global competitiveness will be the development of its human resources. Facing a declining workforce, an aging population, and the loss of its "manufacturing culture," the government is moving quickly to build strong alliances with universities to develop intensive new curriculums in science and technology and to conduct joint research on new technologies.

Japanese industries are moving forward on an aggressive competitiveness strategy of their own—without direct government support or intervention. According to many influential business leaders, government policies are having less effect on private-sector innovation strategies than in the past. Industries are moving quickly to build strong alliances with universities, as well as to harness new technologies, to develop new innovations on original inventions, and to bring them to market quickly in order to remain competitive.

Japanese academia, government officials, industry, and U.S. industry operating in Japan have highlighted various opportunities for greater U.S.–Japan cooperation and business endeavors. Those opportunities represent only a small sample of the many areas of possible cooperation and business development. The examples herein are to provide an illustrative sampling of potential opportunities as seen by leaders in Japan and by multinationals operating in Japan. The samples do not represent an endorsement of a particular entity, opportunity, or policy recommendation.

U.S. Department of Commerce, International Trade Administration

Opportunities highlighted by Japanese companies, officials, and academies, as well as U.S. companies in Japan, include the following:

- Early collaborations between U.S. and Japanese university professors, engineers, and researchers can provide opportunities for U.S. technologies and joint ventures.

- Japan's Center of Excellence programs can be a launch pad for greater U.S.–Japan involvement and collaboration on academic research.

- Japan and the United States could collaborate closely on nanotechnology, particularly in the area of standards development.

- A new bilateral initiative focusing on innovation could lead to collaborations in energy, health, and environment—thus exploring drivers such as access to venture capital, entrepreneurship, protection of intellectual property rights, commercialization of R&D and technology transfer.

- Harmonization of regulations and standards could help facilitate trade between the two countries and aid in the operation of U.S. companies in Japan.

- Because there is significant consumer market demand in Japan in the health-care sector, trained health-care professionals, services, and products will be needed.

- U.S. software services could be pursued in the Japanese market to meet the software needs of technology-driven companies.

- Environmental testing services could be a significant growth market. The United States is ahead in this arena and could continue to be a strong leader in the Japanese market.

Introduction

This report contains insights from interviews with various Japanese academics, Japanese government officials, Japanese industry representatives, and representatives of U.S. companies operating in Japan. The conducted interviews are not meant to be an exhaustive list nor a scientific survey. Time, availability, and travel limitations affected which entities were interviewed. Meetings with various representatives were conducted to gain first-hand insight on the happenings of the manufacturing sector of Japan. Within just four weeks, a snapshot or glimpse of what is happening in the manufacturing arena emerged.

From nearly 100 pages of handwritten notes taken during interviews, this report presents only a sampling of case studies that represent the views of those interviewed. A list of interviewed entities can be found in Appendix B. While the interviews and research were conducted before the financial and economic crisis in fall 2008, many of the insights and lessons learned remain pertinent and timely. Japan's efforts to enhance its competitiveness and to advance its economy have become even more relevant.

Overarching Themes

Five themes illustrate the current state of Japan's efforts to enhance its competitiveness and advance its economy:

1. Japan is engaged in a cohesive "innovation program" at all levels—academia, government, and industry.

2. Japan's science and technology and its manufacturing competitiveness strategic roadmaps are inextricably linked and well funded.

3. Japan's key to global competitiveness will be to develop its human resources.

4. Japanese industry is moving forward with an aggressive competitiveness strategy without direct government support or intervention.

5. Japanese leaders are thinking about how to advance the country's strategic and commercial relationship with that of the United States.

"Innovation 25" Initiative: Looking Ahead to 2025

The first theme is engagement by Japan in a cohesive program at all levels of government and industry to regain what momentum was lost during the economic downturn years.[2] This program can be summed up in one word: innovation. The "Innovation 25" project was launched in 2006 to develop a strategic policy roadmap for the next two decades; it is geared toward "maintain[ing] dynamic economic growth in the face of a declining population with aging society,[3] [and] it is critical to empower Japan's economy through 'innovation' and an 'open' attitude."[4] According to Japan's Innovation 25 strategy, for the country "to become a truly innovative society, the national policies and corporate strategies must be internationally credible, science-based, not precedent-based; and the assessments, reasoning, and valuation of public vs. private investments and cost-effectiveness must be documented."[5]

Japan sees innovation as playing an important role in improving productivity, which will drive its economic growth and global competitiveness, while empowering the nation to contribute to world growth. This can prove especially important given Japan's lagging productivity figures. In 2005, for instance, Japan claimed the lowest productivity rates among industrialized nations, trailing the United States by nearly 70 percent.[6] These discouraging numbers are a direct reflection of Japan's service sector, which consistently receives poor marks. In addition to encouraging innovation as a remedy for poor productivity, the Japanese government plans to focus on deregulation to assist small businesses and to make better use of information technology.[7]

Innovation does not mean technological invention and renovation only, but rather a broad social transformation brought through the results of ideas, discoveries, and invention and with the creation of new social systems and values.[8] Japan's policies to achieve innovation include (a) using global environmental issues as an engine for economic growth and international contributions, (b) doubling investments for education, (c) reforming universities, (d) increasing investments in science and technology, (e) reviewing regulations and social systems with the aim of promoting innovation, and (f) establishing mechanisms within the government to drive Japan as an innovation-oriented nation.

U.S. Department of Commerce, International Trade Administration

The Innovation 25 project will guide specific program initiatives. In 2007, the government of Japan began funding and building "world class research institutes." Japan's Ministry of Education, Science, and Technology (MEXT) is supporting the "World Premier International Research Centers Initiative" (WPI), which aims to maintain five world-class research institutes with US$4 million to US$7 million of funding for each institute per year for 10–15 years.

MEXT also initiated the 21st Century Center of Excellence (COE) program, creating 274 centers between 2002 and 2004 with funding of about US$1.1 million per year for five years for each project, totaling US$1.5 billion. The program is designed to "cultivate a competitive academic environment among Japanese universities by giving targeted support to the creation of world-standard research and education bases."[9] The budget for 2007 was approximately US$186.6 million for on-going grants, and the New Global COE program starting in 2007 had a budget of US$133.5 million.[10] The New Global COE program will focus on improving human capital in a global context.

Strategic Roadmaps: Science, Technology, and Industry Linked Together

The second theme is the link between the Japanese government's science and technology (S&T) strategic roadmap and the country's manufacturing competitiveness strategy. These two are inextricably linked, well coordinated, and well organized; are consistent in policy direction; and are very well funded. Japan has promulgated an S&T strategy that is a driving force throughout the country at all levels. Now in the third phase, the Science Basic Plan focuses on research and development (R&D) and new manufacturing processes. The plan is focused around eight priority areas: life sciences, information and communication technology, environmental sciences, nanotechnology and materials, energy, manufacturing technology, infrastructure, and frontiers (outer space and oceans). The total

budget for R&D for 2007 was estimated to be US$137.9 billion (university research US$26 billion, public research US$14.6 billion, and private companies US$97.3 billion).[11]

The United States, from business and government sources, spent more than US$284 billion on R&D for 2003. For the same year, Japanese R&D expenditures from both sources equaled US$114 billion. Although the United States spent more than Japan in absolute value, Japan's R&D total expenditures as a percentage of gross domestic product (GDP) at 3.2 percent was greater than that of the United States at 2.6 percent.[12] More of Japan's total expenditures were sourced by business enterprises (74.5 percent) than by the government (20 percent). Similarly, R&D expenditures in the United States were also sourced more by business enterprises (63 percent) than by the government (31 percent).[13]

The overall strategy according to Japan's basic plan is to maintain various research funding levels according to the development stage of R&D, to build a sustainable and progressive industry–academia–government collaboration, to promote the use of new technologies in the public sector, and to promote entrepreneurial activities and R&D ventures by private enterprises.[14] Though a significant amount of R&D is being invested and patents are being issued, there is a general belief that "when compared to [that of the United States], the investment of R&D does not always generate profits, and [when compared to that of] other countries, human interaction is not sufficient."[15] Programs such as the New Energy and Industrial Technology Development Organization (NEDO), a government R&D funding agency, are working to forge a stronger link between increased spending on R&D and increased profits. NEDO has introduced a new system for companies in which they must demonstrate how the R&D will lead to innovations if they are to qualify for R&D grants.[16]

The promotion and commercialization of R&D is recognized as the basis for improving manufacturing competitiveness. According to the government's most recent "Monozukuri [which literally means the making of things] White Paper,"[17] innovation is cited as the cornerstone of economic growth, and improvements in scientific knowledge and technology development are seen as essential. In addition, Japan sees minimizing the effect of environmental and population constraints as being necessary to achieve manufacturing competitiveness.

Japan hopes to increase its manufacturing competiveness by harnessing the investments in R&D through aggressive commercialization programs and by strengthening collaborations and partnerships among academia, industry, and government. This concept is known as the "Innovation Highway Concept—Public–Private Sector Collaboration." Development focus areas include rare metal substitution, newly designed airplanes and rockets, next generation robots, nanotechnology basic research, effective Internet search systems, advanced medical technologies, and next generation fuel batteries.[18] These focus areas and strategies are directly linked to the Science Basic Plan. Finally, Japan sees enhancing labor mobility, attracting foreign direct investment and talent from overseas, and creating new markets as key to achieving greater competitiveness.

Human Resources and Education: Investing in People

As for the third theme, Japanese government experts stated that the key for innovation will be to develop human resources and people: "… people who think, plan, and execute. [Thus,] the more international experiences and exchanges and the more opportunities for Japan's youth, the easier and more natural it will be for Japan to become a truly Open Society."[19] This is one of the key goals of the Innovation 25 initiative.

Japan believes that its universities must be reformed to become places where young people from various countries—with different backgrounds and with high aspirations—can share their talents. The government believes that achieving sustainable growth even when the population is declining will require improving levels of productivity and well-being in society through collaboration and cooperation with "non-Japanese" and "non-conventional" Japanese people. Japan sees creating new all-English universities, such as the one in Okinawa, as fostering the kind of international collaboration that will be key to realizing this goal. The doctoral program in materials science and engineering at the University of Tsukuba admits approximately one-half of its students from abroad, and seminars are conducted in English.

The National Institute for Materials Science initiated a bold reform by opening its doors to talented researchers from around the world in 2003, and it created the International Center for Young Scientists (ICYS) with the support of MEXT. Efforts continue to expand this new ICYS system to other research institutes in Japan.[20]

The internationalization of Japan's universities and research centers is part of the government's overall innovation strategy. For instance, Japan's largest public R&D management organization for promoting the development of advanced industrial, environmental, and energy technologies is New Energy and Industrial Technology Development Organization (NEDO). NEDO is working on international projects that range from focusing on efficient energy usage to engaging in international cooperative research programs.[21]

Another force driving this trend toward a more English-speaking society is the competitive challenge of Asia. In India, China, and much of Asia, English is the common international language; therefore, Japan knows that it too must be able to converse in English. For the Japanese, language barriers must be overcome to be a dominant competitive player in Asia.

A Different Kind of Industrial Policy and Competitiveness Strategy Led by the Private Sector

The fourth theme is that, contrary to popular belief, Japanese industry is moving forward on an aggressive competitiveness strategy of its own, without direct government support or intervention. According to many influential business leaders, government policies are having less effect on private-sector innovation strategies than they have had in the past. Facing the competitive pressures from China, a declining workforce, an aging population, and a loss of "manufacturing culture" or sense of *genba*,[22] industries are moving quickly to build strong alliances with universities to harness new technologies, to develop new innovations on original inventions, and to bring them to market quickly. According to a leader in analytical instrumentation, "[D]eveloping innovative technologies and working together with universities at the prefectural level such as the Ishikawa Science Park (industry–academia–government collaboration) will be key to our future success."[23]

With the growing use of robots on the shop floor, researchers and engineers are replacing production line workers. According to a global leader in robotics, approximately 30 percent of Japanese employees are now engineers.[24] Using basic research to develop new technologies, private companies are relied on to discover potential applications. With the exception of small and medium-sized enterprises (SMEs), private companies are no longer getting direct supports from the government (Ministry of Economics, Trade, and Industry or MEXT) to develop products. It is the universities, national labs, and research institutes that receive support. Moreover, with the new Technology Licensing Organization (TLO) law, professors at the universities are able to create their own companies without government approval. This change is a major shift from the past.

According to the various global leaders, Japan should strive to become a post-service economy, with the challenge being to shift to value creation and strategic sectors. These leaders believe that firms at the top should continue to innovate to maintain their competitive lead, as opposed to diversification. Many manufacturers are making strategic decisions to retain their integrated manufacturing processes operations in Japan, while shifting their modular, less high-tech processes to other Asian countries.[25] In other words, manufacturing decisions are made with a long-term focus. This focus is, in essence, the concept of "localization" within the globalization framework.[26]

Given Japan's declining and aging population, firms are focusing on increasing productivity growth through skills upgrading—that is, human resource development. Japanese firms believe that focusing on customer needs, production quality, delivery systems, and the details remain the cornerstone of manufacturing excellence and competitiveness. This emphasis keeps top salaries manageable: the average annual salary of chief executive officers rarely exceeds US$1 million.

U.S.–Japan Economic Partnership

According to government, academic, and industry sources in Japan, focusing on the country's relationship with the United States with regard to overall strategy—within both the public and private sectors—is of utmost importance and comes at a critical time, for many reasons. While the rest of the world seems preoccupied with China, India, and other emerging economic powers, Japan is moving steadily forward on all fronts to address what it sees as significant internal challenges in the areas of demographics, energy, and environment, as well as the competitive threat posed by China and the rest of Asia. Since its recovery from the 10-year recession, Japan's economy has been steadily growing. The country's GDP in 2007 equaled US$4.38 trillion, up 2.1 percent from 2006, which was up 2.2 percent from 2005.[27, 28]

The alliances and partnerships that were formed between the United States and Japan following World War II have matured over the past 63 years. As the United States embarks on implementing free trade agreements with numerous partners, Japan is also forming multiple "economic partnership agreements."[29] Many people in both countries are calling for a U.S.–Japan initiative. In November 2006, the U.S.–Japan Business Council (USJBC) issued a policy statement, which concluded that the most effective and lasting way to revitalize U.S.–Japan economic relations is through a comprehensive, binding economic partnership agreement.[30]

The USJBC urged former Prime Minister Shinzo Abe and former President George W. Bush to take the initiative to get this process started by agreeing to start exchanging information and ideas about the specific outlines of a comprehensive, high-level economic partnership agreement as soon as possible. The leading U.S. business organization in Japan, the American Chamber of Commerce in Japan has made this agreement a focal point since April 2006. Nippon Keidanren and Keizai Doyukai, Japan's most influential business organizations, have also urged the governments to move forward on this issue. Nippon Keidanren and a major U.S. business organization, the Business Roundtable, also endorsed a comprehensive economic partnership agreement in a January 2007 joint statement.[31]

Insights from Japan:
Case Studies—Shared Perspectives

The following case studies further highlight the major themes identified earlier. [32] These case studies are based on first-hand interviews and meetings with various Japanese academics, government officials, and industry representatives. These case studies are illustrative examples of the thinking of various parties interviewed and represent their views alone. The case studies are summaries of opinions and views expressed during interviews and are not personal interpretations or conjectures.

The case studies do not represent an endorsement by the U.S. Department of Commerce of any opinions or positions expressed by the parties interviewed. Additionally, the Department of Commerce does not endorse any particular company or industry identified in the case studies.

Academia's Teachings

Dr. Takahiro Fujimoto, Tokyo University[33]

Dr. Takahiro Fujimoto heads an initiative that fuses academia with manufacturing gurus and engineers. This new program at Tokyo University (funded in part with government support) is attempting (a) to transfer and preserve technical manufacturing know-how from factory floor workers and managers who have recently retired and (b) to avoid losing their unique skills and knowledge.

Overview of manufacturing in Japan: According to Fujimoto, manufacturing in Japan began to change in the 1980s with a new focus on product development and performance integration, which was embodied by Toyota's concept of integrated manufacturing. There were historical underpinnings for this kind of teamwork of multiskilled workers, with management

knowledge coming out of the World War II period that was then focused on manufacturing. Although there were shortages of everything but knowledge, technology know-how and design were in abundance.

With some of the structural problems coming out of the post-war period, Japan learned that, in the manufacturing sector, companies were more likely to face competition and, therefore, needed to constantly improve their production process to succeed. Fujimoto believes that those concepts of integration and continual improvements in production processes spearheaded expertise in Japan's manufacturing sector, and they continue to be key elements of their competitiveness strategy today. For example, Toyota has embodied the idea of improving its production process and, therefore, places heavy importance on the quality of its supplier companies. Fujimoto sees this approach as one way by which Toyota has maintained competitiveness within the automotive field.

Japan's comparative advantage in today's highly competitive world, according to Fujimoto, is its integrated product mechanisms and architectural designs in the manufacturing process. As its population declines and much cheaper wages can be found in continental Asia, Fujimoto sees Japan as having to continue to focus on increasing its local personnel productivity through advancements in the manufacturing process and labor force skills. He believes that the key to Japan's future competitiveness will be to continue to outsource "modular," or more simple products (e.g., refrigerators, TVs, rice cookers), and to retain manufacturing products requiring a sophisticated level of coordination, engineering design, and technology (e.g., robotics, scientific instruments, autos, machine tools). To him, Japan's future strength is based on this fundamental principle. He believes that Japan should continue to produce where it is designing, a principle known as design-based production. Factories should be built where there is market demand, knowledge, information flows, synergies, and strong supplier relationships.

Government Perspectives

Ministry of Economics, Trade, and Industry

Helping not directing the manufacturing industry: Today, the Ministry of Economics, Trade, and Industry (METI) is more market oriented and gives fewer directives on industrial policies than it did historically. Private companies are now developing best practices and leading the way on innovation and industrial policy. However, there are some exceptions, because METI and the government still create directive policies on manufacturing more broadly for small and medium-sized enterprises (SMEs).

Additionally, the Japanese government has broad manufacturing policies in place, which are spelled out in the annual Monozukuri (Manufacturing) White Paper developed jointly by the Labor, Science, and Industry ministries. One major aspect of the government's industrial policy concerns the need to address human capital challenges that are facing the nation through immigration reform, innovation, and education. METI officials see Japan as facing these challenges: an aging population, a declining birthrate, a loss of value for *monozukuri*, and the lack of a skilled workforce.

If Japan is to address the issues of a declining, aging population and a shrinking workforce, officials believe that Japan needs to revise its immigration policy. Immigration reform that is designed to open up the country to foreign workers is being stressed by businesses across Japan. Many consider opening doors to Malaysia Mexico, the Philippines, and Singapore as a key to Japan's sustainable economic growth.

The government is also helping to encourage innovation and new technological developments through support of research and development (R&D) projects.

The Japanese government is also focusing on how to improve the skills of its workforce, in particular to meet the needs of the manufacturing industry. The government is working on investing in the human resource development of its population. To ensure that the workforce is adequately prepared to work in Japan's high-tech manufacturing sector, officials believe there needs to be greater collaboration between universities, technical schools, and industry so that a new curriculum can be built that will meet the specific needs of the manufacturing industry. Furthermore, universities in Japan do not attract foreign researchers, and this absence needs to change, according to METI officials interviewed.

Global strategy: METI officials believe that Japan needs to continue to focus on global markets and a global strategy. They also believe that two of the key elements for a global strategy are (a) diversifying production locations and (b) negotiating free trade agreements. The best example of the benefits from diversifying production locations is in the automotive sector. During the 1980s, Japanese auto firms faced trade restrictions on automobiles and auto parts that were being produced in Japan and then exported to the United States. Because of the limitations on auto exports, Honda and Toyota started U.S.–based productions. In 2000, the Japanese automobile industry started production in China. Production is now split almost equally between Japan and foreign markets, with about 10 million vehicles produced in Japan and 10 million produced in foreign markets each year. This switch has helped Japan become a global manufacturing giant.

A similar yet slightly different situation occurred in the textile industry. Japan's strategy was to allow lower-skilled, lower-quality production to "just go to China" and to keep "higher, end niche factories" in Japan. According to officials at METI, another major tool to promote a global strategy is the negotiation of trade agreements or economic partnership agreements. Japan has laid the foundation for negotiations or has completed agreements with Chile, Mexico, and Singapore, as well as the Association for Southeast Asian Nations.

New Energy and Industrial Technology Development Organization

Changes in regulations help spur collaborations: In the late 1990s, the Japanese version of the Bayh-Dole Act was passed, known as the Technology Licensing Organization (TLO) Act.[34] The government of Japan studied the U.S. government's Advanced Technology Program (ATP) and relevant U.S. laws. Then it passed its own equivalent laws. With changes to the legal structure, industry and universities could cooperate more. Before 2003, most research universities were national, having been established by the government. The old structure of universities created after World War II limited university professors and research centers to collaboration with industry, and it prevented them from directly commercializing any scientific discoveries. If Japan were to enhance and promote industry and university cooperation and innovation, many believed that the legal structure needed to be changed. The TLO did just that, chiefly by allowing university researchers to commercialize and develop their scientific discoveries. Representatives of the New Energy and Industrial Technology Development Organization (NEDO) who were interviewed believe that greater cooperation between industry and universities has resulted in increased R&D on manufacturing-related issues.

Government support of R&D: The government helps to spur research and development through a variety of mechanisms, including NEDO, which promotes R&D that individual private enterprises alone are incapable of implementing. Two-thirds of NEDO's budget goes to research projects. NEDO's participation enables widespread collaboration among industry, universities, and public research organizations, and it provides financial support from public funding. NEDO provides the seed money, organizes the projects, and then turns the actual research responsibilities over to industry and universities.

NEDO's goal is to improve basic research in special fields that industry is interested in. NEDO is currently supporting 18 programs stemming from eight priority areas (electronics and information technology; machinery systems technology; aircraft and space technology; nanotechnology and materials technology; biotechnology and medical technology; chemical substance management; fuel cell and hydrogen technologies; and new energy, energy conservation, and environment technologies). The areas of research that NEDO supports are often related to cutting-edge technology and scientific research, which are risky projects that industry or universities alone could not afford to examine. With research developments often being applicable to multiple fields, leaders at NEDO believe there is a high need for the coordination of all of their activities. As part of an effort to ensure that its funding is being used productively, NEDO has an evaluation (benchmarking) scheme for its funded projects, which is carried out by the Department of Evaluation. Most projects are for a five-year period. NEDO has a staff of more than 1,000 to evaluate results from the collaboration and consortiums that it funds.

Trade Association View

Japan Machine Tool Builders Association

Strengths of Japan's manufacturing sector: Japan Machine Tool Builders Association (JMTBA) representatives believe that Japan's strengths in manufacturing come from a focus on quality and excellence in production and process innovation. Japanese companies may not invent a product; yet through innovation, they improve its production and quality. Innovation in manufacturing is being driven by companies. Japanese government manufacturing policies may not have much to do with private-sector or industry innovation activities. However, while METI is implementing its *monozukuri* project, the Japanese are very focused on baby boomer retirements and the dwindling of *monozukuri* or craftsmanship, as in the culture of manufacturing.

Production process: Production process innovation is essential to improving competitiveness. The Kaizen System, an innovation strategy process at Toyota, was a private-sector initiative and has become the crown jewel, according to JMTBA. The Kaizen System is based on common strategic improvements. The competitiveness model is totally dependent on the Toyota Production System. According to JMTBA representatives, focusing on improving the production process and the quality of products has become a key feature of the Japanese manufacturing sector. If Japan is to improve quality in a factory, JMTBA leaders believe that the company must focus on the shop floor. Every element of the shop floor must be attended to: the engineering quality must be advanced, and there must be a high use of computers. Even the shop floor must be clean and tidy, because this cleanliness will enable problems to be discovered more readily.

Successful Japanese manufacturing companies also stress the importance of multitasking by individuals and of having groups working together to make improvements to existing processes. To JMTBA, there must be an effective and immediate feedback system inherent in the process. Additionally, JMTBA representatives believe that the Japanese mindset is *micro no gainen*, or microscopically conceptually oriented—that is, conservative with great attention to detail.

Challenges to Manufacturing Competitiveness

Government policies: Government policies—particularly corporate law, accounting law, and taxation—affect corporate profitability and, therefore, competitiveness. For the first time in 77 years, the government has made revisions to its tax policies (amortization). JMTBA representatives see this move as a major step in reducing

burdensome policies. At the same time, they believe that the government is still slow to make additional changes in those areas.

Other countries: The association sees competitiveness challenges coming from foreign countries, where companies have begun to focus on producing quality products that will be competing against some of Japan's top products. For example, Hyundai (South Korea) has been improving the quality of its cars and will soon be competing even more with Toyota. Additionally, other countries' companies have realized the importance and success of Japanese companies' processes and are examining how those processes can be used in their own production systems. This analysis is occurring particularly in India.

Lessons from Industry

Historical Perspective and Industry Overview

Consolidated from multiple interviews, many themes emerged regarding the history and perspective of Japanese companies. Many successful manufacturing companies in Japan today were originally involved in basic manufacturing, including textile and *tatami*-mat making machinery. Students studying in the universities during World War II and immediately after developed a tremendous amount of discipline, creativity, and ingenuity.

After the war, those students and academics traveled the world, eager to learn and apply new technologies, and eventually they became some of the leading industrialists in Japan. After World War II, Japanese companies were not allowed to make things of a military nature. As a result, Japanese companies imported U.S. and European industrial machinery, and they were forced to learn how to take the machines apart in order to repair and retrofit them to extend their lifespan, their utility, or both. This process enabled Japanese companies to understand how the machines worked, and thus they learned how to make the machines better. In fact, many Japanese companies were first founded on U.S. or European technology. The Japanese then improved the product and its production process. The government's historically strong connection with Japanese industry enabled the collective strategy and policies that produced the "Japanese Miracle."

Today, the Japanese government has little or no direct role in shaping the nation's industrial sector, with the exception of SMEs. Global leaders in the manufacturing sector are charting their own course and are relying less on directions or funding from the government. Their success has come from adherence to a range of policies, including a continual focus on innovation. Manufacturing companies have worked to continue to innovate their products and production process, maximizing efficiency and functionality.

Top Japanese manufacturing companies claim their success comes from attention to detail, cleanliness, quality, and customer service. Additionally, Japanese companies have stayed focused on their core products, and they do not often deviate or diversify into other areas or investment possibilities. They see this focus as helping them to improve and advance their core product lines. They see the hands-on management style as being another quality of successful manufacturing companies. Many of the founders of these companies have maintained an active role in their companies to this day, acting as grandfather figures. Furthermore, top-level managers remain connected to their employees through their hands-on hiring practices and employee programs, such as Toyota's employee suggestion system. Those companies also practice the idea of *genchi genbutsu*, or go and see the real thing, with top managers conducting frequent site visits and walking around the shop floors.

FANUC: Robotics Global Company

The FANUC "Bible": Dr. Eng. Seiuemon Inaba is the founder and current chair of FANUC. Originally a division within Fujitsu that was dedicated to computer controlled machine tools, FANUC broke off in 1972 to focus on several key

areas, including robotics. The company partnered early on with General Electric, including a joint venture that lasted for more than 20 years. FANUC also partnered with General Motors. Those partnerships, along with relations with various European Union firms, enabled FANUC to stay abreast of technology developments and to become a global leader in industrial robotics and automated machine tools.

Much of Inaba's inspiration for FANUC came from a Tokyo University professor who went to work at the University of California–Berkeley in 1956. The professor sent Inaba and his colleagues at Tokyo University some research papers from the Massachusetts Institute of Technology (MIT) regarding numerical controlled machine tools. The MIT report provided Inaba with the inspiration for his future work, and he refers to it as the "FANUC Bible."

Innovation is key: FANUC officials who were interviewed believe that R&D is central to its business model. One-third of all FANUC employees are engineers. More than 1,000 researchers operate in 11 laboratories. With a pledge to stay focused on its core mission and not to invest in outside areas, FANUC believes focusing on improving its computer numerical control[35] and robotic technology is key. According to company officials, innovation at FANUC has not been hindered by domestic regulations created by the government. In fact, the regulations have even helped to spur innovation. According to FANUC representatives, innovation is key to staying competitive and to meeting challenges that arise from the fast pace of changes in knowledge.

Although technical information was formerly relevant for about 10 years, now it is relevant for only a short time, because technology is changing so quickly. Therefore, the company believes that training is essential. FANUC's innovation depends on people who will stay "motivated" and on the quality of engineering. If FANUC is to maintain leadership, there must be consistency.

For staying ahead in the machine tools area, officials interviewed believe companies need to be working with machine tools for a long time—they need the "failure experience" to improve and stay competitive.

Meeting demand: Japan's aging population, declining workforce, high taxes, and high wages have made labor-intensive production difficult. FANUC officials believe that all hardware production should be done in Japan. Therefore, they are investing in basically unmanned systems to compete with cheap labor overseas. The robot cell, a huge technology-driven system, requires only one human operator during the workday and is extremely reliable. Floor managers and engineers can view the system from their home computer or even their cell phones to make sure operations are running smoothly. FANUC's Robotic Cell Plant is producing about 2,000 robots per month, while using only 80 workers on the actual manufacturing floor. The rest of the manufacturing is done by other robots—robots making robots.

Meeting global challenges: Although market conditions are strong, increases in crude oil prices and uncertainties in the Chinese economy will necessitate taking "precautionary actions to avoid any adverse trends in the business cycle. Under current conditions, FANUC will place even greater emphasis on R&D efforts. This increased R&D effort will be key to FANUC's future success in launching highly reliable, functional, lower-priced, and competitive products into the global marketplace."[36]

Toyota

The Toyota Production System (TPS) has several key aspects: "just in time," *kanban* (literally meaning a signboard or sign), multiskilled workers, an employee suggestion program, and *jidoka* (man and machine working together to ensure that no defects are passed on).

"Just in time" does not mean "just in time delivery" but "just in time sales." The goal is to keep stock inventory as low as possible, which, in turn, keeps costs low. Keeping pace with sales means knowing what is sold, when it is sold, and in what amounts. Therefore, companies know what is needed, when it is needed, and in what amounts for production. The precondition for this just in time method of operation is having "leveled production."

The *kanban* system is another key element of TPS and was first developed in 1963. Every two hours, the *kanbans*, or inventory cards that are located on the supplies boxes or trays at a point of assembly, are collected. Those cards, which identify specific parts, are scanned, and the information for the cards is directly communicated to suppliers so that they know when it is time to deliver additional parts. As a result, supplies are ordered as used (as needed), yet before they are completely depleted. The *kanban* system ensures a constant, steady flow of supplies, but it also ensures that there is no extra inventory; this approach keeps costs down and maintains a steady supply chain.

TPS also includes using multiskilled workers. By educating workers about the whole production process, other workers' mistakes are quickly revealed, given the overlap in skill and know-how. To ensure that no defect is sent on to the next assembly station, Toyota has a "line-stop" system, which can be used with no penalty to a worker. In addition, improvements to the production system come directly from workers' ideas through the employee suggestion system. Employees have suggested more than 640,000 ideas, and virtually all have been adopted.

Another key concept is known as *jidoka*, human productivity improvement and quality assurance. *Jidoka* is embodied in many of the other elements of TPS, including multiskilled workers and the "line-stop" system. According to Toyota officials questioned on the topic, Toyota faces the challenge of finding and developing well-trained people who can use the TPS system to reduce costs.

Relationships with suppliers: Of Toyota's operation, 80 percent is based on suppliers (about 1,000 total) located in Aichi Prefecture. Toyota believes that the physical location of the 1,000 suppliers is important. The key to success is educating suppliers on the *kanban* system and *gishiken* (literally, technical expert) system. Toyota uses this concept of "mother plants," which support a number of subplants and suppliers. As a result, Toyota officials interviewed believe it is essential to train suppliers regarding Toyota's TPS concepts and its safety and quality standards. Ensuring the loyalty of those suppliers and their commitment to Toyota's standards is critical, but it is also strictly voluntary. Toyota's Supplier Support Center provides technical skill development to suppliers. One of Toyota's overseas manufacturing challenges is ordering the quality and quantity of supplies it needs for its TPS system.

Mazak Trading Company

Not just cheap labor: Mazak representatives believe that for a company to stay competitive, it must produce high-quality products using efficient production processes. It must also be continually focused on future innovations and developments in production methods. Overall, Japanese companies are looking to maintain a competitive edge, and they do not think they can do that just by moving to the cheapest labor supply. Much of manufacturing today is done with high-tech machinery that must be run by skilled employees.

The key to ensuring competitiveness for Mazak is to focus on the productivity of workers, not just wages. Mazak has been able to take advantage of the need for high-quality supplies and parts for manufacturing of numerous items, which cannot be found from low-cost, low-skilled labor in places such as China. As manufacturing firms move to places where the high-tech parts cannot be made internally, Mazak supplies those companies with the parts for their operations.

Mazak employees believe that if a company has an original technology and a competitive edge, it should continue to stay in Europe, Japan, or the United States. They believe there is no sense in moving to China only for cheap labor when the production of a product is based on the use of sophisticated technology, which is built from a high expenditure of R&D.

Other additional problems, such as intellectual property right concerns, currency issues, and export controls, also affect a company's decision not to relocate to countries with low-labor costs. Many products, including those produced by Mazak, are subject to government-imposed export controls for China, but not for the United States and Europe. If the company were to relocate to China or even Singapore, it would be required to obtain licenses.

Ensuring productive workers: Mazak employees believe that in order to reduce the cost of manufacturing, companies must be more productive and must maintain a quality advantage. In addition to improving the production process through innovation, staying competitive means having highly productive workers, along with advanced technology. Therefore, maintaining a skilled work force is essential.

Mazak officials also believe that manufacturing companies in Japan attract top engineers because of the cultural value placed on manufacturing. Working in manufacturing in Japan denotes the same social status as working in medicine or law, which is not always the case in the United States. Salary increases are not part of the philosophy that drives Mazak's operation; at the same time, Mazak will not lay off workers. A problem will arise if a company focuses only on hiring qualified workers and does not focus on training. Mazak officials interviewed see companies as needing to engage young people and to promote the manufacturing sector as an employment opportunity. With recent fears of jobs moving to low-wage countries, workers themselves are intent on keeping manufacturing in Japan, and they are committed to improving their companies and the manufacturing sector in Japan.

U.S. Companies That Succeed in Japan

What does it take to succeed as a U.S. company in the Japanese marketplace? Though differences in industries and products make every company's experience unique, common themes and trends can be found. Those themes and trends come from conversations with various U.S. firms operating in Japan. First and most important, U.S. manufacturing companies must adapt to the Japanese way of manufacturing and producing. The Japanese market places a heavy emphasis on quality products, with attention to detail given top priority. Furthermore, Japanese producers who use inputs from American companies want a seamless transition from individual components to a finalized product.

Adapting to the country's heavy focus on a highly effective production process that creates quality specialty products is key for U.S. companies. Successful U.S. companies have also worked to strengthen their customer services—from working with customers, to designing specific products, to end-user assistance.

Examples of U.S. Companies in Japan
Gleason Asia Co., Ltd.
The machine tool industry: Gleason is a wholly U.S.-owned gear-cutting tool manufacturer. Historically, American and European firms dominated the metal-cutting machine tools industry. However, the U.S. tool industry has been in decline for many years and has been trying to reduce costs. In the United States, there is no demand for maintaining a viable manufacturing base; as a result, companies are sourcing parts from outside the United States.

In Japan, there is a large array of good manufacturing companies that are potential customers. This potential, coupled with the fact that Japanese tool machine suppliers have reduced costs and improve training, has enabled the suppliers to remain competitive. Japanese machine tool companies are even manufacturing products in the United States to supply the American domestic market. In Japan, the machine tool market is about 1.4 trillion yen (US$11.9 billion) of which 60 percent is supplied domestically, while 40 percent is supplied from imports. Of the demand for machine tools in Japan, 60 percent comes from the auto sector.[37] In Japan, as in the United States, the machine tool industry is made up of small and medium-sized enterprises.

What is the secret to Gleason's success in Japan? According to representatives of Gleason, Japanese customers want their supply chains to be seamless and will accept nothing less than top-quality products and excellent customer support. Producing high-quality products that meet customers' needs has been a key focus of Gleason. Customers also expect their suppliers to solve any problems quickly and, above all, to focus on Japanese customer needs. Meeting demands from customers has enabled Gleason to develop strong relations and presence in the industry.

Customer interaction and support, including excellent technical knowledge, is key. As a result, Gleason has 60 employees working in sales and customer service in Japan. Gleason officials in Japan believe that a company's U.S. headquarters needs to understand the Japanese culture. This understanding is especially true for Gleason, because there is no manufacturing of their products in Japan. By focusing on technical knowledge and advantage, gear design, and embedded software, plus given the difficulty of transferring this knowledge, Gleason has stayed competitive with its production in the United States despite the shrinking U.S. machine tool industry.

Comparisons between U.S. and Japanese companies: Gleason representatives believe that Japanese companies are more flexible in meeting the standards of their customers. To do so, they focus on attention to detail in the production process, follow up with maintenance, and are willing to reduce profits to satisfy customers.

Harley-Davidson, Japan

What is the secret to Harley-Davidson's success? The motorcycle industry in Japan is very competitive, but Harley-Davidson's success has been based on selling the product. Harley-Davidson employees questioned about the company's success believe that for American products to sell in the Japanese market, the manufacturer needs to have customer satisfaction, top-quality details, marketing excellence, and the concept of localization (or fitting in with the local market).

In Japan, companies need to focus beyond just manufacturing a product. For the motorcycle industry, the after-sales service and strong sales and dealership channels are essential. With high costs for a single unit, excellent customer service at all ends of the spectrum is essential. In Japan, customer satisfaction comes from focusing on the smallest of details. Additionally, for customers who are the end users, treating the sales channel as a family is essential. Harley-Davidson's marketing strategy is developed chiefly by its Japanese office so the company can focus on the unique elements of the Japanese market.

According to the Harley-Davidson Japan representatives, the company focuses on selling the American spirit and its love for big motorcycles. It carries out a big event every year to bring the "Harley-Davidson culture" to Japan. The marketing campaign combines the Japanese mind with the American spirit, as well as Japanese culture with American country and western music. In most cases, the American brand is very appealing to the Japanese, but it also must be tailored. Harley-Davidson believes that, at times, many companies are simply pushing the globalization policy without fully understanding the localization angle.

Boeing, Inc., Japan

Japanese aerospace industry: Boeing has had a long-standing, cooperative relationship with Japan. Boeing Commercial Airplanes has worked closely with the Japanese aerospace industry since 1969. Other segments of Boeing have been working with Japanese firms for more than 50 years. Boeing has played a strong supportive role in developing the Japanese space industry since 1970. Boeing is a leading provider of commercial jetliners to Japanese airlines, a major supplier of military equipment and aircraft to the Japanese Defense Agency, and a significant customer of—and partner with—the Japanese aerospace industry.

Japan has been the largest single-country international market for Boeing Commercial Airplanes in dollar value since the very beginning of the jet era. Japan's aerospace industry is small with total annual sales of only US$9 billion to US$10 billion, with the industry importing more than it exports. Yet aerospace is considered extremely important and strategic to the Japanese economy. Because Japan has stringent export control laws, it depends on working with foreign companies and suppliers. Japan's aerospace sector is a major supplier of components and subsystems to foreign original equipment manufacturers, such as Boeing, Airbus, Bombardier, Embraer, General Electric, and Rolls-Royce.

Boeing's partnerships in production: Japan is the second-largest source of commercial aircraft components for Boeing. Approximately 85 Japanese firms are working with Boeing in various aspects. The Japanese aerospace industry has helped design and build the 737, 747, 767, 777 (supplying 20 percent of the 777 airframe value), and now the 787 (supplying 35 percent of the airframe). Japanese companies are basically moving up the value chain, with Boeing's Japanese partners now designing, marketing, sourcing, and taking on more risk-sharing in product development.

According to Boeing officials in Japan, Boeing's business model in the Japanese aerospace market is based on finding excellent technology suppliers to partner with for every component of an airplane. Boeing has adopted a "just in time" shipping model, which was borrowed from the Toyota Production System model. The shipping model and TPS model have enabled Boeing to assemble the 787 Dreamliner in only three days, compared to 20 days for the 777.

On July 8, 2007, Boeing rolled out the first 787, which Boeing officials claim as a great example of strategic cooperation and partnership. The Dreamliner reflects the importance with which Boeing views the Japanese market and its technological capability. Japan has been willing to invest in new state-of-the-art plants and new autoclaves to facilitate the 787's production, in spite of the fact that Japan has a relatively small domestic industry.

Mitsubishi Heavy Industries,[38] Kawasaki Heavy Industries, and Fuji Heavy Industries have been working with Boeing for more than 30 years on the development of the 767 and the 787. Those companies supply fuselage panels, aerodynamic fairings, landing-gear doors, and inspar ribs.

U.S. Department of Commerce, International Trade Administration

Opportunities for Greater U.S.–Japan Relations

Various Japanese academics, government officials, industry officials, and U.S. companies operating in Japan have highlighted opportunities for greater U.S.–Japan cooperation in government and business endeavors. Twelve challenges and opportunities are listed next as illustrative samples of potential opportunities seen by Japan and multinationals operating in Japan. These examples do not represent endorsements of a company, an opportunity, or any specific policy recommendations.

Academia

1. Challenge for Japan: There is a lack of engagement by U.S. researchers with Japan.

Opportunity for the United States: Forming early collaborations between U.S. and Japanese university professors, engineers, and researchers could provide opportunities for U.S.–developed technologies, products, and joint ventures. Professors collaborating to develop different applications with the same technologies can be vital to success. China is now sending researchers to Japanese research institutes because of visa restrictions for travel to the United States. Japanese collaborations and long-term alliances with China in the areas of nanotechnology, quantum physics, and information technology are being formed.[39]

Opportunity for the United States: The Centers of Excellence program, with its international focus, could be a launch pad for greater U.S.–Japan involvement and collaboration. Japan is seeking to make its research institutions world class. This move could provide an entry point for U.S. access.[40]

2. Challenge for Japan: Japan's university curriculums do not meet the emerging needs of its industries.

Opportunity for the United States: Japan's universities need to be reengaged with industry, so that curriculums are more closely linked to needed applied research and future technology development. Closing the gap between universities and industry on techniques to commercialize research and development (R&D) and technology transfer will be essential to fully harness the benefits of R&D. This area is where collaboration between the United States and Japan could be mutually beneficial. Universities also need to attract foreign researchers. This is an area where perhaps the United States can share best practices of effective programs and collaborative initiatives, and it will require participation of government and industry.[41]

Government

3. Challenge for Japan: Japan wants to be a leader in nanotechnology development.

Opportunity for the United States: Nanotechnology will be a linchpin for manufacturing competitiveness. Japan and the United States could collaborate closely on the nanotech front to develop standards conforming to the International Organization for Standarization. Infrastructure challenges and intellectual property protection are issues that should be considered.[42]

4. Challenge for Japan: Japan needs to increase venture capital and to reduce regulatory barriers in order to promote life sciences research.

Opportunity for the United States: Collaboration in the energy/environment/health areas could be helpful in the future in order to examine barriers to development. In Japan, there are few venture capital firms in the life sciences in comparison to the United States, because of the perceived high risk in investing in this sector. Japan is focusing on regulatory issues associated with life sciences, and it has set up a special commission to work with industry and universities. The United States could be involved in this initiative.[43]

5. Challenge for Japan: Japan has a shrinking population and workforce.

Opportunity for the United States: Immigration reform to open up Japan's doors to foreign workers is being stressed by businesses across Japan. The declining population and aging workforce will be serious problems in the years ahead, and the change will require significant immigration reform to offset the effects. Emphasis on English as a common language in Japan could help to attract more overseas talent and collaboration, particularly with the United States.[44]

6. Challenge for Japan: Regulatory barriers in Japan impede market access and competition.

Opportunity for the United States: Harmonizing regulations and standards, obtaining greater clarity on Japanese labor policies, and protecting intellectual property rights are key areas of focus from the perspective of U.S.-based companies manufacturing in Japan.[45]

7. Challenge for Japan: There is a lackluster U.S.-Japan economic partnership.

Opportunity for the United States: A new bilateral initiative, similar to a free trade agreement but not focused on tariffs, is being called for by some. They see the focus of such an initiative as being on innovation, environment, energy, intellectual property rights, secure and seamless trade (port security), standards and regulations, rules for mergers and acquisitions, and foreign direct investment.[46]

Industry

8. Challenge for Japan: With an aging population, there is a need a for strong health-care sector in Japan.

Opportunity for the United States: There is significant consumer market demand in Japan in the health-care sector. Trained health-care professionals, services, and products will be needed. Health-care costs are also growing significantly, with individuals now having to cover a greater percentage just as Japan's budget for medical services is shrinking. (Japan's expenditures on health care are equal to 8 percent of gross domestic product, compared to 15 percent of gross domestic product (GDP) in the United States.)[47] The upgrading by universities, research organizations, and medical institutions of their equipment could provide market opportunities for U.S. products and services.[48]

9. Challenge for Japan: Japan needs to meet the software needs of technology-driven companies.

Opportunity for the United States: U.S. software services could be pursued aggressively in the Japanese market. Most of Japan's manufacturing base is using U.S. software to make their designs. Because none of the big companies are using Japanese software, few companies are developing software. Consequently, the Ministry of Education, Science, and Technology and the Ministry of Economics, Trade, and Industry are working on issues such as interoperability (including a US$1.1 billion investment), thereby creating infrastructure in industry, creating government simulations, and developing the next generation of supercomputers.[49]

10. Challenge for Japan: Japanese companies always need new and better suppliers in a globalized economy.

U.S. Department of Commerce, International Trade Administration

Opportunity for the United States: There are opportunities for U.S. firms to get their products into Japan and into the Japanese production lines, but a certain business model has been suggested by U.S. firms currently operating in Japan. The model includes becoming "Japanese" as soon as possible; joining trade associations; hiring locals; seeking to be viewed as an "insider"; avoiding the "table-pounding" approach; being willing to "study and learn first, then teach"; and establishing strong relationships with the staff at the U.S. Embassy.[50]

11. Challenge for Japan: Japanese companies are looking to measure environmental impacts.

Opportunity for the United States: Environmental testing services will be a huge growth market—

particularly in measuring small particles. The United States is ahead in this arena and could continue to be a strong leader in the Japanese market.[51]

12. Challenge for Japan: Japanese companies face varying global standards and regulations on automobiles.

Opportunity for the United States: In the automotive sector, harmonizing fuel efficiency standards and regulations among the United States, the European Union, and Japan could ultimately help to improve U.S. competitiveness around the world.[52]

Appendix A. Overview of Japan's Economy and Manufacturing Sector

Japan's blazing economic growth of the 1980s came to a halt with its stock market crash in 1990. A recession plagued the country for the next 10 years. Japan had fully recovered from the recession by 2004. In 2006, the economy grew by 2.2 percent with domestic (particularly private) consumption, non-residential investment, and external demand contributing to the growth. Japan's gross domestic product (GDP) in 2006 was US$4.36 trillion. Exports are a major component of Japan's GDP accounting for 15 percent of GDP in 2006, with goods exports totaling US$647 billion.[53] The United States is Japan's largest export market.

Manufacturing has been a key element of Japan's economy since the beginning of the post–World War II period. The manufacturing sector accounted for 21 percent of the nation's GDP in 2004, an increase from its 2003 contribution level.[54] Manufacturing exports from Japan equaled US$510.7 billion in 2006, which accounted for 80 percent of the country's total goods and services exports. Although the United States' manufacturing exports, which equaled US$924 billion, were larger than Japan's in absolute value as a percentage of total exports, the manufacturing exports for the United States at almost 64 percent were much lower than Japan's manufacturing exports as a percentage of total exports.[55]

Japan's manufacturing sector also employs a significant portion of the country's total labor force.[56] Though declining slightly in recent years, the manufacturing sector in 2005 employed almost 17 percent of the country's total work force. According to an Organization for Economic Cooperation and Development (OECD) report, Japan has the second-largest manufacturing sector behind the United States, but it is significantly above the number three country, China. In 2002, the Japanese manufacturing sector equaled around US$800 million. The United States manufacturing sector equaled around US$1,400 million.[57] In 2005, Japan had almost 470,000 manufacturing enterprises.[58] In 2002, the United States had more than 350,000 manufacturing enterprises.[59]

Throughout 2005, the stock of U.S. foreign direct investment (FDI) in Japan equaled US$75.5 billion, significantly up from only US$68.1 billion in 2004. The U.S. FDI in Japan is mostly in the finance sector, manufacturing, wholesale trade, and professional and technical services.[60]

Although total FDI in Japan had been growing, FDI by 2005 accounted for only 2.4 percent of GDP in comparison to the United States, where FDI accounted for 15 percent of GDP. FDI in the United States in 2005 equaled US$1.6 billion, of which 12 percent was from Japanese investors. Investment by Japan in 2004 accounted for almost 1 percent of private-sector GDP and for 614,000 workers in the United States.[61] Japanese foreign-owned industries in the United States are mostly in the transportation machines, chemicals, food and agricultural processing, machines, and electronic sectors.[62]

In Japan's strong manufacturing sector, foreign-affiliated companies have played a valued role. There were 463 foreign affiliates in the manufacturing sector in Japan, of which 175 were U.S. owned. This figure compared to a total of 468 Japanese affiliates in the United States.[63] In 2004, 4,272 total foreign affiliates were in Japan, of which 17.6 percent were in the manufacturing sector.[64] Manufacturing foreign affiliates accounted for

US$24.5 billion in exports in 2003,[65] which was almost 5 percent of total goods exported from Japan that year.[66] Foreign manufacturing affiliates in Japan employed almost 165,700 workers in 2003.[67]

According to a survey of foreign affiliates in Japan, a majority of foreign affiliates surveyed saw the Japanese market favorably, and more than half of the survey companies planned to expand their operations in Japan.[68] Japanese manufacturing firms have also gone overseas and have set up foreign affiliates, especially within the United States. Japanese foreign affiliate manufacturing plants are set up across the country, with the greatest number of Japanese manufacturing plants being in California, followed by Ohio, Illinois, and Georgia. The greatest number of Japanese foreign affiliates in the United States are found in the transportation machine parts industry, followed by chemical and oil products, food and agricultural processing, machinery, and electronic/electrical parts.[69]

Table A.1: Key Economic Indicators of Japan and the United States, 2006

Comparing Economies: Japan and the United States		
Indicator	Japan	United States
GDP (US$ billions)	4,360	13,246
Total exports (goods and services; US$ billions)	647	1,037
Exports as a percentage of GDP	15	8
Manufacturing exports (US$ billions)	510.7	924
Manufacturing exports as a percentage of total exports	80	63
GDP per capita (US$)	34,188	44,190
Investment as a percentage of GDP	24.1	20
FDI as a percentage of GDP (2005)	2.4	15

Source: Japan External Trade Organization, World Trade Organization, Economic Intelligence Unit, and the International Monetary Fund.

Table A.2: Manufacturing Foreign Affiliates in Japan and in the United States

Manufacturing Foreign Affiliates in Japan				
	2002	2003	Percent of Total Manufacturing Foreign Affiliate Activity by U.S. Manufacturing Foreign Affiliates, 2002	Percent of Total Manufacturing Foreign Affiliate Activity by U.S. Manufacturing Foreign Affiliates, 2003
Number of Enterprises				
Total manufacturing foreign affiliates	419	463		
U.S. manufacturing affiliates	168	175	40.1	37.8
Number of Employees				
Total manufacturing foreign affiliates	123,127	165,693		
U.S. manufacturing affiliates	38,663	65,060	31.4	39.3
Total Exports (billions of US$)				
Total manufacturing foreign affiliates	19.12	24.55		
U.S. manufacturing affiliates	3.17	5.21	16.6	21.2
Value Added (billions of US$)				
Total manufacturing foreign affiliates	16.19	20.88		
U.S. manufacturing affiliates	4.58	8.71	28.3	41.7
R&D Expenditure (billions of US$)				
Total manufacturing foreign affiliates	3.19	4.09		
U.S. manufacturing affiliates	0.55	0.30	17.4	7.4

Manufacturing Foreign Affiliates in the United States				
	2002	2003	Percent of Total Manufacturing Foreign Affiliate Activity by Japan Manufacturing Foreign Affiliates, 2002	Percent of Total Manufacturing Foreign Affiliate Activity by Japan Manufacturing Foreign Affiliates, 2003
Number of Enterprises				
Total manufacturing foreign affiliates	1,768	1,703		
Japan manufacturing affiliates *	491	468	28.0	27.0
Number of Employees				
Total manufacturing foreign affiliates	2,236,400	2,117,400		
Japan manufacturing affiliates	326,400	310,600	14.6	14.7
Total Exports (billions of US$)				
Total manufacturing foreign affiliates	88.5	87.8		
Japan manufacturing affiliates	12.7	14.4	14.4	16.4
Value Added (billions of US$)				
Total manufacturing foreign affiliates	229.2	220.6		
Japan manufacturing affiliates	28.9	29.1	12.6	13.2
R&D Expenditure (billions of US$)				
Total manufacturing foreign affiliates	20.1	21.0		
Japan manufacturing affiliates	1.2	1.1	6.0	5.3

Source: OECD, *Measuring Globalisation: Activities of Multinationals, Manufacturing*, (Paris: OECD, 2007). *www.oecd.org/document/37/0,3343,en_2649_33703_38763813_1_1_1_1,00.html.* Figures for investment in Japan originally were in Japanese yen. Conversions are based on an exchange rate of 126.36 yen per US$1 in 2002 and 118.33 yen per US$1 in 2003.

*Data provided by the Bureau of Economic Analysis, U.S. Department of Commerce

Appendix B. Meetings and Contacts

Acknowledgements:

The authors would like to express their sincere appreciation to the following individuals who provided direction, insights, and support for this project. Without their help, this project would not have been possible.

Government

International Economic Affairs Division and Trade Policy Bureau of the Ministry of Economics, Trade, and Industry (METI)

Atsuo Kuroda, Director

Takashi Mogi, Assistant Director, Americas Division

Noriyuki Mita, Director, Americas Division

Yoshiko Shimayama, Assistant Chief

Takayuki Niikura

Technology Promotion Division of METI

Takayuki Sumita, Director

Manufacturing Industries Bureau of METI

Kenichiro Urakami, Principle Deputy Director, Automobile Division

Agency for Natural Resources and Energy of METI

Jun Arima, Director, International Affairs Division

Financial Services Agency

Matsuda Naokoi, Director for Enforcement of Corporate Disclosure

National Institute for Material Sciences

Masahiro Takemura, Deputy Director, International Affairs Office

National Institute for Advanced Industrial Science and Technology

Naoyuki Taketoshi

New Energy and Industrial Technology Development Organization

Masahiro Hashimoto, Director General, Policy Planning and Coordination Department

Embassy of Japan, Washington

Atsushi Taketani, First Secretary, Economic Section

Academia

Manufacturing Management Research Center, University of Tokyo

Takahiro Fujimoto, Executive Director and Professor of Economics

Research Institutes

Asian Technology Information Program

Todd Tilma, Technology Analysts Japan

David Kahaner, Founding Director

RIKEN Genomic Sciences Center, Yokohama Institute

Hiroshi Hirota, Deputy Project Director, Protein Research Group

Industry

Varian Technologies

Kunio Aoi, Senior Manager, Scientific Instruments

Mitsuo Seki, Group Manager, Scientific Instruments

Kenny Watanabe, President

Sumitomo 3M

Hideo Nozu, Vice President, Technical and Corporate Environment Management

Yoshiaki Okano, Senior Manager, Customer Technical Center

Toshiki Shibata, Senior Manager, Marketing

Shigeru Yoshida, Manager, Marketing

Junichi Tanaka, General Manager, Traffic Safety Systems Division

Harley-Davidson, Japan
  Katsuya Masuda, Deputy Department Manager, Sales Promotion/Communications
  Toshifumi "Tomi" Okui, President
  Toyoki Fukumori, Department Manager, Presidential Staff Room

Gleason Asia Co., Ltd.
  Michiharu Chikano, President
  Kiyoshi (Dennis) Iguchi, Executive Officer, Machinery Marketing Department, Tools Sales Department, Overseas Marketing Department
  Michihior (Mike) Nomura, Managing Director, Sales Administration Department, Financial Control and Administration Department, Ishibashi Musical Instrument Company

Toyota Motor Corporation (Aichi)
  Kenji Miura, General Manager, Operations Management Consulting Division
  Rie Kitahashi, Corporate Public Relations Division

Toyota's Motomachi Assembly Plant, Toyota Kaikan Display Center (Nagoya)

Mori-Seiki Co., Ltd. (Nagoya)
  James Nudo, Manager, Legal Department
  Mari Yamamoto, Marketing Strategy Department

Shimadzu Corporation (Kyoto)
  Shingo Takimoto, Managing Corporate Officer, Manufacturing
  Ken Emori, General Manager, General Planning Department, International Marketing Division
  Shigeaki Fujimoto, General Manager, Manufacturing, Analytical and Measuring Instruments Division
  Teruo Kato, General Manager, Manufacturing and Logistics Strategy Department
  Takeshi Kawamoto, Senior Marketing Manager, Scientific and Industrial Equipment Department, International Marketing Division

Horiba Inc. (Kyoto)
  Nobuhiro Tanji, Department Manager, Corporate Strategy Office
  Yuichi Muroga, Corporate Officer, International Division

Yamazaki Mazak Trading Corporation (Nagoya)
  Kazuo Nishimura, Managing Director, Overseas Sales and Marketing Headquarters
  Motoyasu Kakutani, Manager, Sales Division, Europe, North and South America

Mazak Minokamo Plant (Nagoya)

FANUC Ltd. (Mt. Fuji)
  Dr. Eng S. Inaba, Founder and Honorary Chairman
  Shinsuke Sakakibara, Honorary General Manager and Senior Development Engineer
  K. Kohari, Senior Managing Director
  Joji Abe, Manager, Secretary Division

General Motors Asia Pacific (Japan) (Shinagawa)
  Antonio (Toti) Zara, President, Vehicle Sales
  Rick Brown, President, Operations and Representative Director
  Toshio Horiuchi, Director, Technology Research, Public Policy, Industry and Government Relations

Ford Japan Limited
  Randy Krieger, President and CEO

Daimler Chrysler Japan

Proctor and Gamble Japan
  Tadasi Otsuka, Manager, External Relations
  Makoto (Mark) D. Kawai, Specialist, Regulatory Trade Association, Central Government Relations and External Relations

Boeing Japan
  Gary Konop, Director, Government Relations

GE Medical Devices
  Abby Pratt, Government Communications Manager, Government Market Development

Trade Associations

Japan's Machine Tools Importers Association
  Michiharu Chikano, Chair

Japan Tool Builders' Association
  Kunio Tsugami, Director, International Marketing Department

American Chamber of Commerce Japan and Automobile Industry Subcommittee
  Clemence Mayali, Manager, U.S. Government Affairs

Clemence Mayali, Manager, U.S. Government Affairs

Masataka Toyota, Staff Director, Medical Devices and Diagnostics Subcommittee

U.S. Embassy, Tokyo, Japan

John Peters, Minister-Counselor for Commercial Affairs

Patrick Santillo, Counselor for Commercial Affairs

Hisanao Aomori

Joshua Handler

Tamami Honda

Dean Matlock

Yukari Minowa

Catherine Spillman

Hisao Tamada

Larry Weber, Director, National Science Foundation Tokyo, Regional Office

Rie Yamaki

U.S. Consulates

Nagoya

Daniel Rochman, Principal Officer

Michihiko (Mitch) Yokoi

Osaka

Chikako Akai

Comparison of R&D Expenditures between Japan and the United States

Table C.1: Comparison of R&D Expenditures between Japan and the United States

R&D spending in Japan and the United States			
Indicator	Year	Japan	United States
Gross domestic expenditure on R&D as a percentage of GDP	2005	2.60	3.30
Total GDP expenditure (US$)*	2005	287.8 billion	115.1 billion
R&D expenditure by source of financing, percentage share in national total	2006/2005		
Government		29.30	16.80
Business Enterprise		64.90	76.10
Other national sources and foreign sources		5.80	7.10
Business enterprise sector R&D expenditure as a percentage of value added in industry	2005	2.60	3.40
Business R&D espenditure (US$)	2003	196.1 billion	85.5 billion
Share of government-financed business R&D	2003	4.00	0.80
Government R&D expenditures as percentage of GDP	2005/2003		
Civil		0.50	0.70
Defense		0.63	0.00

*Figures are adjusted to purchasing power parity for the U.S. dollar in 2000.

Source: OECD, Main Science and Technology Indication Database, May 2007; OECD, R&D database, May 2005.

U.S. Department of Commerce, International Trade Administration

Abbreviations and Acronyms

ASEAN   Association for Southeast Asian Nations

ATIP   Asian Technology Information Program

ATP   Advanced Technology Program

CNC   computer numerical control

COE   Center of Excellence

EPA   Economic Partnership Agreement

FDI   foreign direct investment

GDP   gross domestic product

ICYS   International Center for Young Scientists

JMTBA   Japan Machine Tool Builders Association

METI   Ministry of Economics, Trade, and Industry

MEXT   Ministry of Education, Science, and Technology

MIT   Massachusetts Institute of Technology

NEDO   New Energy and Industrial Technology Development Organization

OECD   Organization for Economic Cooperation and Development

R&D   research and development

S&T   science and technology

SME   small and medium-sized enterprise

TLO   Technology Licensing Organization

TPS   Toyota Production System

USJBC   U.S.–Japan Business Council

WPI   World Premier International Research Centers Initiative

WTO   World Trade Organization

Endnotes

[1] Many economists agree that 2004 brought an end to the recession that started in 1990. See Appendix A, "Overview of Japan's Economy and Manufacturing Sector," for a summary of Japan's economy and manufacturing trends.

[2] Japan's blazing economic growth of the 1980s came to a halt with the stock market's crash in 1990. A recession plagued the country for the next 10 years. Japan fully recovered from the recession in 2004. See Appendix A for an overview of Japan's economy and manufacturing sector.

[3] Japan's population growth has slowed in recent years, declining sharply since the 1980s. According to the 2005 Census Report, the population was 127.76 million, below the 2004 estimate of 127.78 million. This decline marked the first time since World War II that population had fallen from the previous year. It is expected to shrink at a pace unprecedented for any nation in peacetime. In 2005, the population of elderly citizens (65 and over) was 26.82 million, constituting 21 percent of the total population and marking record highs. (This figure compares to 7.1 percent of the population in 1970.) The percentage of the aging population in Japan is rising much faster than in advanced Western European countries or in the United States. By 2015, the population of elderly will have risen to one in four, or more than 30 million. Statistics Bureau and Statistical Research and Training Institute, Ministry of Internal Affairs and Communications, 2005, "Briefing: Japan's Changing Demography," *The Economist*, July 28–August 3.

[4] Innovation 25 Strategy Council, "Innovation 25 Interim Report," February 26, 2007, p. 1. *www.cao.go.jp/innovation/en/pdf/innovation25_interim_full.pdf*; final report released May 25, 2007, and approved by the Japanese government cabinet on June 1, 2007.

[5] Ibid.

[6] The Nikkei, "Japan's Productivity Only 70% of U.S. in '05: Cabinet Office," Wednesday, April 11, 2007, morning ed.

[7] Ibid.

[8] Innovation 25 Strategy Council, "Innovation 25 Interim Report."

[9] Tokyo Regional Office, National Science Foundation, "Report Memorandum #07-04," May 11, 2007. *www.nsftokyo.org/rm0,-04.pdf*.

[10] Ibid.

[11] MEXT Government Budget Seminar for Academic Scientific Research, January 2007.

[12] See Appendix C; OEDC, R&D database, May 2005; OECD Main Science, Technology, and Industry database.

[13] Ibid.

[14] Government of Japan, "Science & Technology Basic Plan," March 28, 2006. *www8.cao.go.jp/cstp/english/basic/3rd-Basic-Plan-rev.pdf*.

[15] MEXT Government Budget Seminar, 2007.

[16] METI Technology Policy in Japan, February 2007.

[17] METI White Paper on Manufacturing Competitiveness, 2006.

[18] Ibid.

[19] Government of Japan, "Long-term Strategic Guidance Innovation 25," June 1, 2007. *www.kantei.go.jp/foreign/innovation/innovation_final.pdf*.

20 National Institute for Materials Science, International Center for Young Scientists. *www.nims.go.jp/icys/01about/0101.html.*

21 New Energy and Industrial Technology Development Organization (NEDO), 2006, "Profile of NEDO," Saiwai, Japan.

22 *Genba* means "on-the-spot," "at the scene," or "being present on the shop floor." It is what managers are expected to do in manufacturing plants. This concept is embodied in manufacturing excellence.

23 Interview with Varian Technologies, Tokyo, Japan.

24 Interview with FANUC, Mt. Fuji, Japan.

25 Integrated processes are used for the production of items that require many components to be carefully designed to work together to ensure optimal performance. The design of those interrelated items requires teamwork among the research, development, and production components of a company, as well as between producers and their suppliers.

26 Based on interviews conducted in Japan; see Appendix B for list of interviews.

27 International Monetary Fund, World Economic Outlook Database, 2006. *www.imf.org/external/pubs/ft/weo/2007/01/data/index.aspx.*

28 Central Intelligence Agency, *World Factbook*, 2007 estimate. *www.cia.gov/library/publications/the-world-factbook/index.html.*

29 Japan has signed bilateral free trade agreements with Singapore, Chile, the Association for Southeast Asian Nations (ASEAN), and Mexico and has agreed in principle with Australia, Switzerland, and the Gulf countries. Japan also participates in the Asia-Pacific Economic Cooperation forum and various other regional trade groups, such as the Asia-Europe meeting, ASEAN+3, and an East Asian summit. World Trade Organization, "Trade Policy Review: Japan. 2007." *www.wto.org/english/tratop_e/tpr_e/tpr_e.htm;* Ministry of Foreign Affairs of Japan, "Free Trade Agreement (FTA)

and Economic Partnership Agreement (EPA)." *www.mofa.go.jp/policy/economy/fta/index.html*

30 The USJBC called for a comprehensive economic partnership agreement that would significantly cover trade in industrial and agricultural goods, trade in services, non-tariff barriers such as standards and regulations, investment rules, and trade compliance issues. "Revitalizing U.S.–Japan Economic Relations: 2007 Policy Statement." *www.usjbc.org/2007%20 Policy%20Statement%20English-Japanese%20Final.pdf.*

31 Business Roundtable and Nippon Keidanren, "Joint Statement U.S.–Japan Economic Partnership Agreement," January 19, 2007. *www.keidanren.or.jp/english/policy/2007/007.html.*

32 The case studies are based on interviews with various academic, government, and company leaders. The case studies summarize opinions and views expressed during interviews and are not interpretations.

33 Fujimoto is one of Japan's leading authorities on manufacturing competitiveness. He has written numerous books, notably *The Evolution of a Manufacturing System at Toyota* (Oxford: Oxford University Press, 1999). He frequently advises top government officials and leaders.

34 The Patent and Trademark Law Amendment Act of 1980, commonly known as the Bayh-Dole Act, provides for a legal framework for the commercialization of inventions that were developed by universities with the use of federal funding.

35 Computer numerical control (CNC) technology enables machine tools to be operated and controlled by programmed commands stored within a computer. CNC technology is much more efficient than manually controlled machine tools.

36 "FANUC Annual Report," 2006.

37 From an interview with Gleason Asia. Conversions are based on an exchange rate of 117.75 yen per US$1 in 2007.

[38] In March 2008, Mitsubishi Heavy Industries announced that it would be starting production on the first aircraft made in Japan in more than 30 years. Mitsubishi Heavy Industries president, Kazuo Tsukuda, emphasized that government support was essential for the success of the project. Pratt & Whitney, an American company based in Connecticut, will be manufacturing the engines for the midsized jet. This information was announced by Yuri Kageyama in "Mitsubishi Launches Regional Jet," The Associated Press, March 28, 2008.

[39] From interviews with Asian Technology Information Program (ATIP) and Varian.

[40] From interview with National Science Foundation, Tokyo.

[41] From interviews with METI and Sumitomo 3M.

[42] From interviews with ATIP and National Institute for Materials Science.

[43] From interview with Institute for Advanced Industrial Science and Technology

[44] From interview with METI.

[45] From interview with Procter and Gamble.

[46] From interviews with General Electric Medical, METI, and American Chamber of Commerce in Japan.

[47] OECD, "OECD Health Data 2007," October 2007. *www.oecd.org/document/16/0,2340,en_2825_495642_2085200_1_1_1_1,00.html.*

[48] From interviews from Horiba, Inc.; General Electric Medical Devices; and ATIP.

[49] From interview with ATIP.

[50] From interview with General Electric Medical.

[51] From interview with Horiba, Inc.

[52] From interviews with METI, General Motors Japan, Chrysler Japan, and Ford Japan.

[53] Japan External Trade Organization, "Japanese Trade and Investment Statistics." Accessed August 2007, *www.jetro.go.jp/en/stats/*; IMF, World Economic Outlook Database. *www.imf.org/external/pubs/ft/weo/2007/01/data/index.aspx.*

[54] World Trade Organization (WTO), 2007, "Trade Policy Review: Japan," Geneva: WTO. Accessed September 2007, *www.wto.org/english/tratop_e/tpr_e/tp276_e.htm.*

[55] Economist Intelligence Unit, "Country Profile: United States and Japan," 2007. *www.eiu.com.*

[56] METI, "Preliminary Report on Census of Manufacturers, 2005," 2006. Accessed September 2007, *www.meti.go.jp/statistics/kougyou/2005/sokuho/h17s_stat_e.xls.*

[57] OECD, *The Changing Nature of Manufacturing in OECD Economies* (Paris: OECD, 2006).

[58] METI, "Preliminary Report on Census of Manufacturers, 2005."

[59] U.S. Census Bureau, "Annual Survey of Manufacturers—U.S. Census 2005," U.S. Department of Commerce, Washington, D.C., November 2006. *www.census.gov/prod/2006pubs/am0531gs1.pdf.*

[60] U.S. Trade Representative, "2007 National Trade Estimate Report on Foreign Trade Barriers," Washington, D.C., 2007. *www.ustr.gov/Document_Library/Reports_Publications/2007/2007_NTE_Report/Section_Index.htm.*

[61] U.S.–Japan Partnership for Growth. "United States-Japan Investment Initiative Report, 2007," 2007. *www.state.gov/documents/organization/86189.pdf*

[61] JETRO, "JETRO's Annual Survey: Japanese Manufacturing Plants in the U.S." Tokyo, February 2003. *www.jetro.go.jp/en/stats/survey/pdf/2003_02_biz.pdf.*

[62] OECD, *Measuring Globalisation: Activities of Multinationals, Manufacturing* (Paris: OECD, 2007) *www.oecd.org/document/37/0,3343,en_2649_33703_38763813_1_1_1_1,00.html.*

U.S. Department of Commerce, International Trade Administration

[63] JETRO, "JETRO Releases the Results of Its Annual Survey of Foreign-Affiliated Firms in Japan," Tokyo, April 12, 2005. *www.jetro.go.jp/en/news/releases/20050413221-news.*

[64] OECD, *Measuring Globalisation.*

[65] Ibid. Converted to US$ based on 113.3 yen per US$1.

[66] OECD, *Measuring Globalisation.*

[67] JETRO, "JETRO Releases the Results."